LIONS

by Cynthia Overbeck

Photographs by Tokumitsu Iwago

A Lerner Natural Science Book

Lerner Publications Company ▪ Minneapolis

Sylvia A. Johnson, Series Editor

Translation by Setsuko Takeuchi
Additional research by Jane Dallinger

LIBRARY OF CONGRESS CATALOGING IN PUBLICATION DATA

Overbeck, Cynthia.
  Lions.

    (A Lerner natural science book)
    Adapted from Lions by Tokumitsu Iwagō, originally
  published under title: Raion.
    Includes index.
    SUMMARY: Describes the complex and dangerous
  life of lions on the African savannas.

    1. Lions—Juvenile literature. [1. Lions] I. Iwagō,
  Tokumitsu. Raion. II. Title. III. Series: Lerner natural
  science book.

  QL737.C23093   599.74′428   81-1962
  ISBN 0-8225-1463-X   AACR2

This edition first published 1981 by Lerner Publications Company.
Revised text copyright © 1981 by Lerner Publications Company.
Photographs copyright © 1970 by Tokumitsu Iwagō.
Adapted from LIONS copyright © 1974 by Tokumitsu Iwagō.
English language rights arranged by Japan UNI Agency, Inc.
for Akane Shobo Publishers, Tokyo.

International Standard Book Number: 0-8225-1463-X
Library of Congress Catalog Card Number: 81-1962

132346

    4   5   6   7   8   9   10   90   89   88   87   86   85

A Note on Scientific Classification

The animals in this book are sometimes called by their scientific names as well as by their common English names. These scientific names are part of the system of **classification**, which is used by scientists all over the world. Classification is a method of showing how different animals (and plants) are related to each other. Animals that are alike are grouped together and given the same scientific name.

Those animals that are very much like one another belong to the same **species** (SPEE-sheez). This is the basic group in the system of classification. An animal's species name is made up of two words in Latin or Greek. For example, the species name of the lion is *Panthera leo*. This scientific name is the same in all parts of the world, even though an animal may have many different common names.

The next group in scientific classification is the **genus** (GEE-nus). A genus is made up of more than one species. Animals that belong to the same genus are closely related but are not as much alike as the members of the same species. The lion belongs to the genus *Panthera*, along with its close relatives the leopard, *Panthera pardus*, the tiger, *Panthera tigris*, and the jaguar, *Panthera onca*. As you can see, the first part of the species name identifies the animal's genus.

Just as a genus is made up of several species, a **family** is made up of more than one genus. Animals that belong to the same family are generally similar but have some important differences. Lions, leopards, tigers, and jaguars all belong to the family Felidae, a group that also includes cheetahs and domestic cats.

Families of animals are parts of even larger groups in the system of classification. This system is a useful tool both for scientists and for people who want to learn about the world of nature.

Throughout history people have thought of the lion as the "king of beasts." With its huge mane and proud walk, the lion does have a majestic look. But lions do not live the easy lives of kings. They must struggle to survive in the grasslands of their native home.

Today, most lions live on **reserves*** in southern and eastern Africa. (A few lions also live in India's Gir Forest Sanctuary.) Reserves are huge fenced parks, many acres in size. Within these parks, many kinds of wild animals live a protected life in their natural environment. People are not allowed to hunt these animals. Instead, visitors come to such places as South Africa's Kruger National Park and Tanzania's Serengeti National Park to study and photograph lions and other animals as they go about their daily lives.

*Words in **bold type** are defined in the glossary at the end of the book.

The reserves are located in the beautiful African **savannas** (suh-VAN-nahs). These are broad, open areas of tropical or subtropical grassland scattered with trees and shrubs. The savanna is the home not only of the lion but also of two of its closest relatives—the leopard and the cheetah. The lion (*Panthera leo*), the leopard (*Panthera pardus*), and the cheetah (*Panthera onca*) belong to the family Felidae—the cat family. Lions are also closely related to many other types of big wild cats such as tigers and jaguars, as well as to the common house cat.

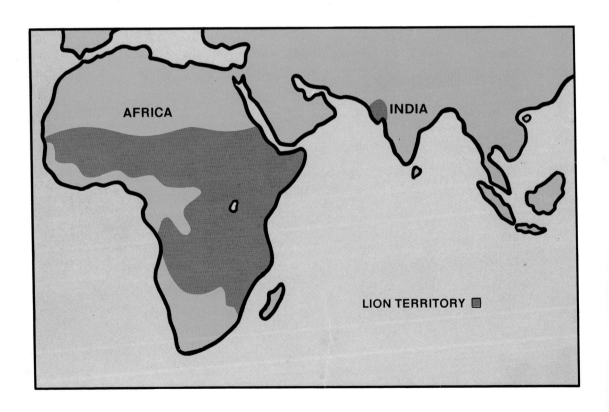

The cheetah   **The leopard**

Lions and other wild cats are **carnivorous** (Kar-NIHV-or-us); that is, they eat meat. In order to eat, they must hunt and kill the animals in their environment. The animals that they hunt for food are called **prey** (PRAY).

The life of a hunter like the lion is not an easy one. Sometimes it is difficult to find and catch prey. If a hunt is unsuccessful, the lion will go hungry. In many ways the lion's life depends on the lives and habits of the animals that it hunts.

The lion hunts many of the animals that share its African home. The prey most often chosen are the zebra, the wildebeest, the gazelle, the impala, and sometimes the wild pig and the warthog. All of these animals are **ungulates** (UN-gyoo-lets), or hoofed mammals. They all feed on plants. Most of them do not have sharp teeth or claws with which to defend themselves. Their only defense is their ability to run fast.

Sometimes, lions will attack the babies of larger plant-eating animals such as the giraffe, hippopotamus, elephant, rhinoceros, and buffalo. Because the healthy adults are big and strong enough to defend themselves, lions usually choose the young, the weak, or the sick to prey upon. This actually helps to keep the herds of these animals healthy and strong. By killing the weak and sick, lions often help to stop diseases from spreading and attacking healthy members of the herd.

Among the many kinds of antelopes that live in the African savannas are gazelles *(above)*, elands *(below)*, and wildebeests *(below)*.

Impalas and zebras are favorite prey animals of lions.

A herd of elephants protects its babies.

The adult rhinoceros *(above)* and hippopotamus *(below)* are two animals that the lion does not often succeed in hunting down.

The lion's body is specially equipped for hunting. The golden-brown color of its fur blends into the surrounding leaves and grasses so that the lion can sneak up on unsuspecting animals without being seen. The lion is also built for speed. Its body has no extra fat, and its strong legs carry it easily through the grasses. When chasing prey, lions have been known to run up to 35 mph (56 kmph) for short distances. The lion's muscled legs and body also give it strength. A lion can leap a farmer's 5-foot (1.5 meter) fence with a whole cow held tightly in its powerful jaws.

In addition to speed and strength, a lion needs sharp senses. Good eyesight, sense of smell, and hearing help the hunter to find and stalk its prey. Lions have the largest eyes of any carnivore. Their eyes are very sensitive to light. This means that lions can see especially well at night, when they do much of their hunting. Lions can judge distances well, and they are quick to spot moving objects. The lion's good hearing and sense of smell also help it to find prey.

The lion's strong paws and sharp, curved claws are useful once the prey is caught. The lion uses its claws to grab the animal and hold it down. The claws work just like those of a house cat. They retract, or pull back, into the paws until they are needed. This helps to keep them razor sharp. If the claws did not retract, they would grow dull from rubbing against the ground.

Lions use their powerful teeth, as well as their claws, to hold and bite prey. The four pointed **canine** (KAY-nine) teeth hold and kill the animal and tear the meat. The other teeth cut through tough skin and bones as the lion eats. Lions do not have any teeth for chewing; they swallow the meat in chunks.

The lion's rough tongue also helps it to eat. The lion uses it to lick hair from the skin of the prey and to scrape meat off the bones. Like house cats, lions also use their tongues to clean themselves and each other.

The lion's teeth, tongue, and claws are used especially for catching and killing prey and for eating. Other parts of the lion's body are used for communication. Close communication is very important to the lion's survival. Lions must cooperate and communicate with each other in order to protect themselves and their babies.

The lion's tail is an important communicator. Adult lions carry their tails high in the air as they move through the tall grass of the savannas. The black tuft on the end of the tail is easy for other lions, especially the **cubs**, or babies, to follow. When a male lion wants to frighten another male or to show off for the females, or **lionesses**, he raises his tail high in the air and struts proudly back and forth. At the same time, he also shows off his beautiful **mane**—the thick hair around his face and neck—by holding his head up high.

Lions use sounds as well as body movements to communicate with each other. Male lions roar loudly to call their fellow lions together or to keep strange animals out of their territory. Lionesses roar more softly to call their cubs. Both make certain growls or coughing sounds when they are about to attack or fight. Like all cats, lions purr when they are contented.

A male lion poses proudly against the grasses of the savanna.

Most male lions, lionesses, and cubs live together in close-knit family groups called **prides**. A pride can include from 4 to 40 animals. Usually, the pride is made up of 2 or more adult lionesses, all of their cubs under 2 years old, and 2 or more adult male lions. The lionesses stay together in the same pride all their lives. They are usually related to each other as sisters, mothers, or daughters.

The males, too, are often related to one another. But they

do not stay with the same pride for life. They may stay for a few months to several years. But at some time, younger, stronger males will come to drive out the older males and take over the pride. These will, in turn, eventually be driven out and replaced.

Each pride of lions has its own **territory**, or area of land. This area may be from 10 square miles (26 square km) to 100 square miles (260 square km) in size.

Within the pride's territory is usually a smaller area where the families spend most of their time. This area includes the best hunting grounds and the best water hole or river, as well as good places to hide the young cubs. When the lions cannot find enough food in this central area, they must go into the outer parts of their territory to hunt.

The pride's territory is carefully guarded. It is the male lion's job to defend the pride and its territory from outsiders. Like dogs, male lions urinate on the bushes and trees in their territory. The smell warns other male lions to stay away. Also, the male lions roar a lot just before sunrise and just after sunset. Their roar at these times is so loud that it can be heard for miles. People who study lions think that this roaring warns strange lions to stay away.

But strange lions often wander into the pride's territory in spite of the warnings. Many times these strangers are **nomadic**, or wandering, lions. They have no special territory, and they do not belong to any pride. They wander about the countryside, alone or with small groups of the same sex. (Nomads can be either males or females.)

Nomads that wander into the pride's territory are safe if they happen to meet a pride member of the opposite sex. But if a male nomad meets one of the pride's males, or a female nomad meets a lioness from the pride, there is usually a fierce fight. One lion is either killed or driven away. Sometimes when two or more nomadic males fight a male pride member, they win the battle and become the leaders of the pride.

A pride's territory is precious. It must be protected because it is the home of the lions' prey. Some lion territory has a good supply of water and many healthy prey animals all year round. A pride with such an area does not need to travel around very much. But in some parts of African lion country, there are two separate seasons—wet and dry. The amount of grass and leaves changes with the seasons. This affects the grazing habits of the lions' plant-eating prey. The prey animals must move about with the seasons, and the lions must follow.

24

Left: **A lioness stalks the grassy savanna.** *Right:* **This male lion's fur blends well with the forest colors.**

From November to May is the wet season in Africa. Then there is a lot of rainfall, and the grass on the plains is plentiful. Many of the lions' prey come to graze on the thick grass. The lions can easily hide in the grass and sneak up on their prey. In these months hunting is good, and the pride stays on the plains. But in May, when the dry season begins, fires start easily in the dry grass. Much of it burns off. The lions' prey then move to woodland areas surrounding the plains. There they find more plants and leaves to eat. The pride follows and sets up home ground by a riverbank near the woods.

Whether on the plains or near the woodlands, the pride's daily life is much the same. When there is a good supply of prey in the area, the lions do not need to spend much time hunting each day. They generally spend about 20 hours a day sleeping or resting. Usually the pride rests on the ground in the shade of a tree. They often lie sprawled next to and even on top of one another. But sometimes they sleep up in the trees to avoid many of the bothersome insects that swarm over them on the ground.

When there is plenty of water, the lions drink once a day, early in the morning or after eating. If they are in a dry area, they can go for nine days or more without water. Then they get their only liquid from the blood of their prey. When they finally do find water, they may drink for 20 minutes without stopping before their thirst is quenched.

Lions can also go for a week or longer without eating if the food supply is scarce. When a lion finally does make a kill, it can eat up to 75 pounds (33.8 kilograms) of meat in one huge meal. But normally adult lions eat about 10 to 15 pounds (4.5 to 6.8 kilograms) of meat a day.

While male lions protect the territory and the pride, it is the lionesses that do most of the hunting. Male lions *can* hunt, but in a pride they usually leave this up to the females, who are in many way better hunters. The males' large manes are too easy for prey to spot. Also, the heavier weight of the males makes them slower than the females.

Lions often hunt in groups. But a lioness working alone can kill a smaller animal, such as a gazelle or an antelope, by surprising the prey. Surprise is important, because many of the animals that the lion hunts are very fast runners. If they sense the lion's presence before the lion can attack, they will take off. Although the lion can run, too, a single hunter usually cannot run fast enough to catch a gazelle or impala that is moving at full speed. For this reason, a lion will rarely attack if it has been seen by a prey animal. The prey seem to know this, for they often graze very peacefully within sight of a pride of lions—at a safe distance, of course.

But if the lioness does manage to stay hidden from the prey long enough to get close, the story is different. When the lioness spots a herd or individual before it spots her, she flattens her body down low into the grass. She begins to creep toward the animal, fixing her eyes on it intently. If the prey gives the slightest sign that it senses danger, she freezes perfectly still. Then slowly, quietly, she creeps closer.

Finally the lioness gets close enough. She charges the prey from behind. With her powerful front claws, she grabs the animal by the neck or hindquarters and pulls it down. When she has forced it to the ground, she bites deeply into its throat and hangs on until the animal dies. She may begin to eat the catch on the spot, or she may drag it into the shade to eat it.

A lioness hunting

Surprise works well for a single lioness, but often teamwork is needed, too. This is why lions frequently hunt in small groups. They do this especially when they are trying to trap a herd on the run, or to bring down a large animal such as a buffalo or a giraffe. As a team, the lions work well together. They spot several giraffes, for example, and spread out quickly and silently around them. If the animals begin to run, several lionesses waiting at different places trap the prey. Once one of the giraffes is caught, it may take two or more lions to bring it down and kill it.

When a large animal such as a giraffe is killed, the whole pride shares the meal. But their manner of doing so is not very polite. The adults often fight over the meat. These mealtime battles can be vicious, and they often result in scars, missing eyes, and other injuries. The males eat first; then the lionesses. Last in line are the young cubs, who must wait until the lionesses have eaten their fill.

Lion cubs generally have a very poor chance for survival. When food is scarce, they may starve to death because the adults will not leave any food for them. Even when there is plenty of food, they may be killed by diseases or attacked by other animals or even adult lions. Sometimes they may be accidentally crushed by an adult rolling over in its sleep. But because a lioness generally gives birth to a litter of one to five cubs every two years, enough cubs survive to keep the lion population going.

A pregnant lioness carries her cubs in her body for about three and a half months. When she is ready to give birth, she finds a protected spot within the pride's home territory. Sometimes she chooses a den in the rocks; sometimes a shelter of trees and bushes. When the cubs are born, they are completely helpless. They weigh only about two to five pounds (about one or two kilograms), and they cannot walk or see. Yet, a few days after they are born, their mother must leave them to begin hunting. The cubs live on milk from her body, but she must continue to hunt for meat to feed herself. During the time that she is out hunting each day, the cubs may be left alone. If some of the other lionesses in the pride also have young cubs, one female adult may stay home from the hunt to watch over all the cubs.

This kind of "day-care" system is another way in which lions in a pride cooperate to help one another survive. The cubs of nomadic lionesses are in for greater danger than cubs in a pride. Usually the mother must leave them completely alone when she goes out to hunt. Their only defense is to hide quietly until she returns. Many of the cubs do not survive. They are killed by hyenas, wild hunting dogs, leopards, or even strange lions. Cubs raised in a pride have a better chance for survival.

The cubs that do survive grow quickly. By the time they
are three weeks old, they can walk fairly well. And by six
to seven weeks, they can follow their mother around easily.
At about this time, their mother brings them out of their den
to join the pride. They soon learn to play with the other cubs
and adults. They even begin to nurse, or drink milk, from
mothers besides their own. Any mother in the pride will
nurse and protect any cub, whether it is hers or not.

At this point in their lives, the cubs are taken for the

first time to a place where prey has been killed. Here, they eat their first meat. As babies, they never had meat —only their mother's milk. Their mother never took meat back to the den because the smell might have attracted enemies. Now, they are beginning to learn their parents' ways of survival.

Like pet kittens, the cubs are very playful. In their play, they practice movements that they will use in hunting and fighting as adults. They chase and wrestle with each other and bite playfully. They may lie watching their mother's waving tail intently, then pounce and try to catch it. At first they are clumsy, but little by little they learn coordination and speed.

When the cubs are about 15 months old and have grown their adult teeth, they are taken out on real hunts. There they learn to stalk prey and to follow their parents' example. By the time they are a year and a half old, they are treated like adults. They are no longer led to kills and cared for by their mothers but must hunt on their own. They look like adults, too. Their fluffy, spotted baby fur has become sleek and golden brown, and their fat bodies have grown long and lean.

At 3 to 4 years old, the young lionesses are ready to have litters of their own. At about the same age, the young males are chased out of the pride to become nomads. They will wander alone or with a few others until they are old enough and strong enough to try to take over another pride. When they are fully grown, they will weigh about 400 pounds (180 kilograms) and will be about 9 feet (3 meters) long, including their tails. Their manes, which are thin and yellow-brown when they are young, will grow long, thick, and dark by the time they are 5 years old. Both the males and females may live to be 20 or 30 years old if they are lucky, but few will survive that long.

Lions are not often killed by other animals. Sometimes a group of hyenas or hunting dogs will attack them. Or lions might be trampled to death while they are hunting buffalo or elephants.

The lion's real enemies have usually been human beings. People have greatly reduced the world's lion population over the years. Two groups—hunters and ranchers—have been largely responsible. In the past, lions were hunted by tourists for sport. They have also been hunted by African tribal people to prove courage and daring.

African farmers and ranchers have also killed many lions. The lions have been driven out as people need more and more land for growing crops and raising livestock. Lions can cause special problems for African cattle ranchers. The ranchers' cattle in their pens are a handy meal for a lion, since they cannot run or defend themselves.

Two young members of the Masai tribe

Especially at night, lions have been known to jump into a cattle pen and kill a cow. Then they leap the fence with the cow and run off to eat it. They have also learned to stampede cattle so that the frightened animals break out of the pens themselves. Then the lions catch them on the run. The ranchers must hunt down and kill the lions to protect their livelihood. One tribe that keeps cattle—the Masai (mah-SI)—are especially brave in hunting down lions. Somehow the lions seem to know this, for they are very careful about stealing from Masai ranches.

Lions on game preserves quickly grow used to tourists' cars.

Generally, wild lions avoid humans. On the reserves in Africa, however, where the lions are safe from human hunters, they have become used to people and cars. They even become friendly. But a lion is never really a tame animal, even when it is born and raised in a zoo or a circus. The instincts of the hunter are always there, and even tame lions can easily turn into killers.

Today, the "king of beasts" no longer roams wild and free over many parts of the world as it once did. But on the reserves in Africa and India, lions still live much as they always have. There they hunt, carrying on the life of the pride and the daily struggle to survive.

GLOSSARY

canine teeth—sharp, pointed teeth used for biting and tearing

carnivorous—meat-eating, as opposed to plant-eating

cub—a young lion

lioness—a female lion

mane—the long, thick hair that grows around the male lion's neck

nomad—a wandering lion that does not belong to any particular pride or territory

prey—an animal that is hunted and killed by another animal for food

pride—a group of lions

reserve—land set aside by people where animals may live in their natural environment. Hunting of animals is not allowed on a reserve.

savanna—tropical or subtropical grassland area with scattered trees and shrubs

territory—an area of land inhabited and guarded by a pride of lions

ungulate—a mammal with hoofs

INDEX